Scott Foresman

Classroom Management Handbook for Differentiated Instruction Practice Stations

Glenview, Illinois • Boston, Massachusetts • Chandler, Arizona • Upper Saddle River, New Jersey

ISBN-13: 978-0-328-47768-5
ISBN-10:　　0-328-47768-0

6 7 8 9 10 V063 14 13 12

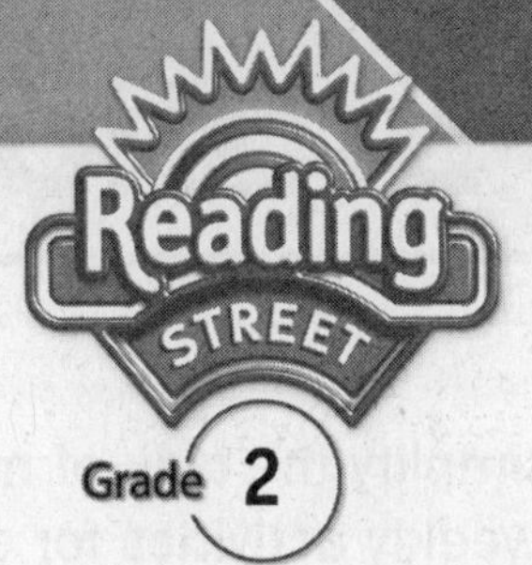

Table of Contents

Welcome to Station Time!

Practice Stations Kit

The Leveled Practice Stations Kit helps simplify the task of managing stations by providing ideas for setting up classroom stations, weekly activities for each station, and suggested materials for each station.

Classroom Management Handbook for Differentiated Instruction Practice Stations

The Management Handbook provides valuable resources to help you set up practice stations and to provide differentiated practice that enables you to address children at their instructional levels while they are working independently. The Scott Foresman Differentiated Instruction Practice Stations help students develop as independent thinkers who take responsibility for their own learning. The Handbook provides a suggested classroom floor plan that can be adjusted to fit the particular needs of your classroom. An overview for each station provides suggestions for setting up the station and essential materials to include. The reproducible Work Plans list tasks that children will complete at each station and help children plan and track their assignments at each station.

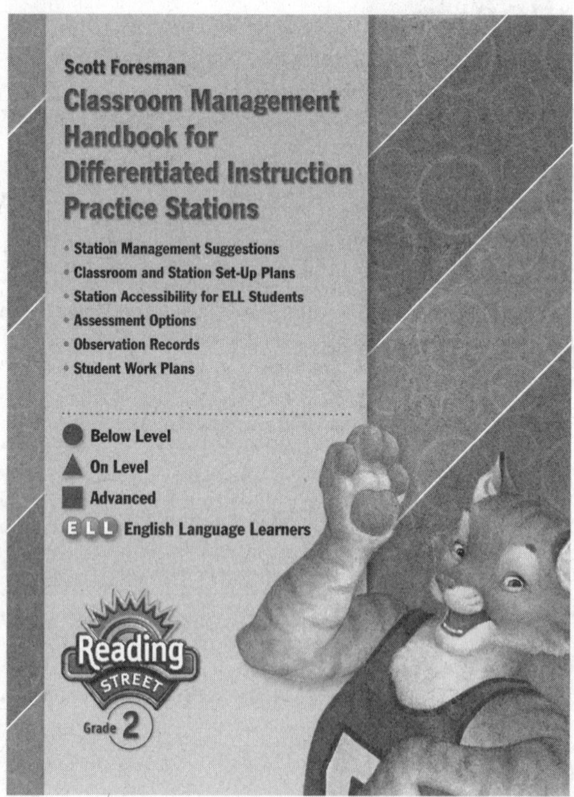

Practice Station Flip Charts

The Practice Stations Flip Charts are tabletop-sized flip charts with the Practice Stations activities from the Teacher's Edition. Each flip-chart page provides the weekly differentiated activities for that station. The activities provide opportunities for children to practice skills and to expand knowledge of the weekly concept. There are six flip charts, one for each station.

- Listen Up!/Word Wise (Phonemic Awareness Station/Spelling Station)
- Word Work (Phonics Station)
- Words to Know (Vocabulary Station)

- Let's Write! (Writing Station)
- Read for Meaning (Comprehension Station)
- Get Fluent (Fluency Station)

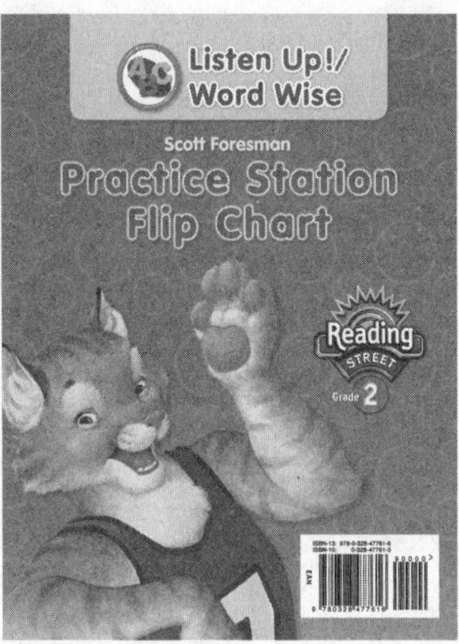

Setting Up the Stations

The classroom environment is an important factor in children's learning. To help create a comfortable environment that is conducive to learning, create separate spaces for the different types of instruction and activities that take place.

How can I set up the stations?

The thought of setting up stations in your classroom can be a bit daunting. This is especially true if you have a small classroom. Making room for stations can be accomplished if you start by thinking of the stations as extensions of your lessons.

- A station does not need to be large. A comfortable pillow in a cozy corner makes a great Read for Meaning station.

- With young children, pick a location for a station and maintain that location throughout the year.

- Set up your stations so that children will not distract those working independently or with you in a small group.

Productive Station Time

By taking time in the beginning to "teach" children the routine for each station, your children will develop as independent learners and the stations will enhance the learning in your room! Have fun with the stations; they are a powerful piece of your curriculum.

- Tell children what types of materials are in each station.

- Tell them what they will practice in each station. Explain the activity options provided in each station if they finish the assigned activity early.

- Model how to use the station and the materials in each station.

- Have children role play for the class appropriate behavior and possible situations they may encounter in the station.

- Explain how "My Work Plan" can help them keep track of the tasks they have completed.

- With young children it is often best to gradually add stations. Too much too soon can be overwhelming.

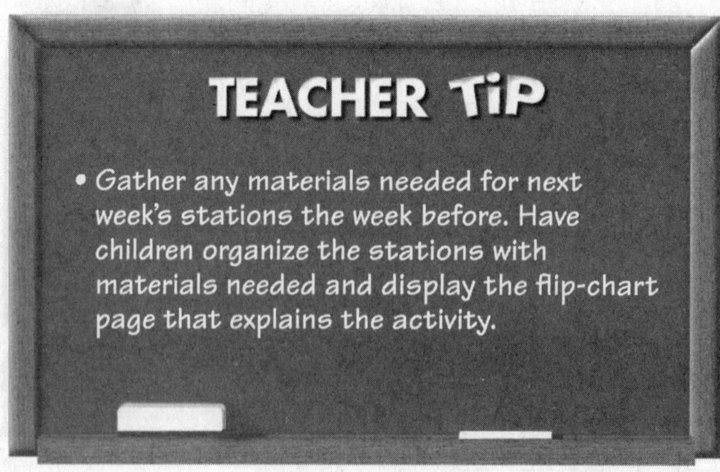

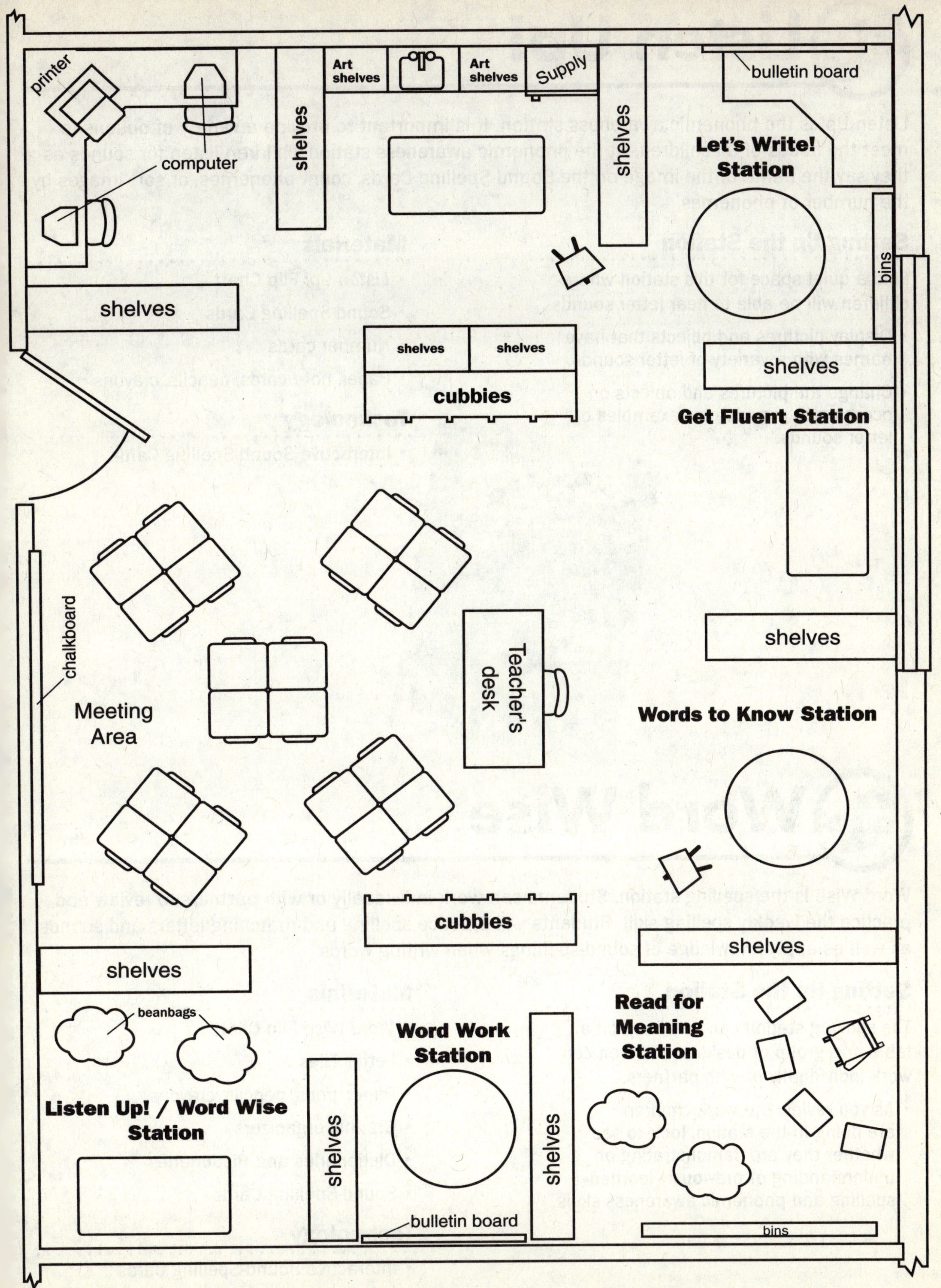

printer
computer
shelves
shelves
Art shelves
Art shelves
Supply
shelves
bulletin board
Let's Write! Station
bins
shelves
shelves
cubbies
Get Fluent Station
chalkboard
Meeting Area
Teacher's desk
shelves
Words to Know Station
cubbies
shelves
shelves
beanbags
Listen Up! / Word Wise Station
Word Work Station
shelves
shelves
bulletin board
Read for Meaning Station
bins

Listen Up!

Listen Up! is the phonemic awareness station. It is important to provide a variety of options to meet the needs of all children. At the phonemic awareness station, children listen for sounds as they say the name of the image on the Sound-Spelling Cards, count phonemes, or sort images by the number of phonemes.

Setting Up the Station

Find a quiet space for this station where children will be able to hear letter sounds.

- Display pictures and objects that have names with a variety of letter sounds.

- Change the pictures and objects on occasion to provide new examples of letter sounds.

Materials

- *Listen Up!* Flip Chart
- Sound-Spelling Cards
- Number cards
- Paper, note cards, pencils, crayons

Technology

- Interactive Sound-Spelling Cards

Word Wise

Word Wise is the spelling station. Students can work individually or with partners to review and practice the weekly spelling skill. Students will practice spelling and matching letters and sounds, as well as apply knowledge of sound-spellings when writing words.

Setting Up the Station

The spelling station can be set up on a table or a group of desks so children can work individually or with partners.

- As you review the work children are doing in the station, look to see whether they are demonstrating an understanding of previously learned spelling and phonemic awareness skills.

Materials

- *Word Wise* Flip Chart
- Letter Tiles
- Paper, pens, pencils, crayons
- Graphic organizers
- Dictionaries and Pictionaries
- Sound-Spelling Cards

Technology

- Interactive Sound-Spelling Cards

Word Work

Setting up Word Work, the phonics station, presents another challenge because of the wide range of abilities among children. You need to have a large variety of materials and options to meet the needs of all children.

Word Work is the station where children will need the most support.

Setting Up the Station

The phonics station is where children can demonstrate what they have learned in phonics by building words with Letter Tiles and then writing the words.

As you review the work children do in the phonics station, look to see whether they are demonstrating an understanding of the phonics skills you have taught.

- Are they applying the target skill?
- Are they also applying previously learned skills to their work?

Materials

- *Word Work* Flip Chart
- Letter Tiles
- Magnetic Letters and Boards
- High-Frequency Word Cards
- Sound-Spelling Cards
- Teacher-made word cards
- Paper and note cards
- Pencils, blue and red markers, crayons
- Sorting baskets
- Decodable Practice Readers
- Write-On/Wipe-Off Boards
- Dictionaries and Pictionaries

Technology

- Interactive Sound-Spelling Cards
- Decodable eBooks
- Online Dictionaries
- Modeled Pronunciation Audio CD

Words to Know

At Words to Know, the vocabulary station, children use various activities to practice and demonstrate their ability to apply the lesson vocabulary skill. Children will also build their speaking and reading vocabularies.

Setting Up the Station

- Supplement the station with other vocabulary-building activities that are language-rich.
- Post previously learned vocabulary in the station and encourage children to use these words when possible.

Materials

- *Words to Know* Flip Chart
- Letter Tiles
- High-Frequency Word Cards
- Envision It! Pictured Vocabulary Cards
- Teacher-made word cards
- Paper, note cards, pencils, crayons
- Sentence sheets
- T-charts
- Magazines, books, catalogs, maps, or other sources of colorful photos and art
- Objects that can be used to provide examples of the vocabulary words
- Dictionaries, Pictionaries, and Glossaries

Technology

- Tested Vocabulary Activities
- Online Dictionaries
- Sing with Me Animations
- Journal Word Bank

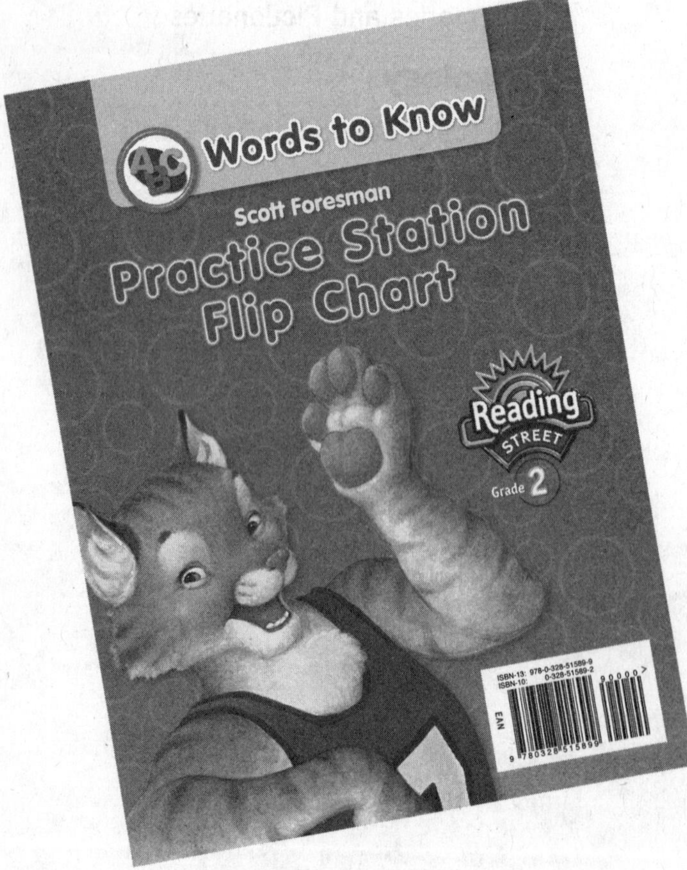

Let's Write!

The writing station is another place where you need to address a wide range of abilities. Children need to begin where they are. The more resources you provide in the station, the more successful it will be for all. As you review the work children do in the writing station, look to see whether they are applying the skill you have introduced. Writing is an excellent way to assess phonetic development.

Setting Up the Station

Let's Write! may need more space than other stations.

- Designate a table for children who are working on prewriting and drafting activities and another for revising, editing, and publishing.

- Set up computers for word processing on another table or on a group of desks.

- Write the Amazing Words and the high-frequency words for the week on index cards and place them in the station. Encourage children to write using Amazing Words and high-frequency words.

- Encourage children to write to their friends.

- Place envelopes and a class mailbox in the station; children can write and mail letters.

Materials

- *Let's Write!* Flip Chart
- Picture Cards
- Pencils, markers, crayons, scissors, glue, glitter, yarn, hole punch
- Magazines, catalogs, or other sources of pictures that can be cut up
- Word banks, dictionaries, writer's handbooks
- Prewriting graphic organizers and revising and editing checklists

Technology

- Grammar Jammer
- Online Graphic Organizers
- Online Journals

Read for Meaning

At Read for Meaning, the reading comprehension station, children can read by themselves or with partners to practice and review the target comprehension skills and strategies. They can make connections across texts, explore personal interests, or find out more about topics, authors, and genres that are related to the weekly concept.

Setting Up the Station

Find a comfortable space for this station away from the main activity of the classroom.

- Include a table and chairs as well as rocking chairs, carpet squares, or beanbags.
- Use shelves, wire rack bins, or plastic tote trays to create an organized classroom library.
- Gradually add and take away books to avoid having too many books, which can overwhelm children.
- Group books by theme, topic, genre, reading level, or author.

Materials

- *Read for Meaning* Flip Chart
- Leveled Readers
- Decodable Practice Readers
- Books by topics and themes
- Books by favorite authors
- Class-made books
- Paper, pencils, crayons
- Graphic organizers

Technology

- Decodable eBooks
- Leveled Reader Database
- Reading Street Leveled Readers CD-ROM
- Envision It! Animations
- Main and Paired eSelections
- Online Graphic Organizers

Get Fluent

Get Fluent, the fluency station, is the place where children will practice fluent reading. Students will listen to and read aloud various texts while focusing on reading with accuracy, at an appropriate rate, with appropriate phrasing, and with expression and intonation.

Setting Up the Station

Children will often read with a partner. Set up this station where the children's work will be the least disruptive to other classmates.

- Locate the station near a computer so children can utilize available technology.

- Provide headsets so that children listening to audio will not be distracted by other noises.

- Arrange the table and chairs to allow partners to work together easily.

- Occasionally reassign partners in order to provide children with a variety of fluency models and partner feedback.

Materials

- *Get Fluent* Flip Chart
- Leveled Readers
- Decodable Practice Readers
- CD player

Technology

- Reading Street Leveled Readers CD-ROM
- Leveled Reader Database
- Decodable eBook
- AudioText CD

ELL-Accessible Stations

The *Scott Foresman Practice Stations* can be adapted to be more accessible to English language learners. Frontloading suggestions and background building information found in the core lesson help support all of the independent activities in the stations. Modeling with picture cues, real objects, and role-playing can help English language learners understand what they need to do without solely depending on language. Children should be encouraged to listen, speak, read, and write during their time in each station. Enhance language production by structuring cooperative learning opportunities at the Practice Stations. Pair children who share the same home language, or have more proficient children work with newcomers. This extra support provides a positive example and support for completing activities in the stations. The stations provide an environment where children can feel comfortable practicing English without worrying about errors they may make.

Listen Up!/Word Wise and Word Work

Listen Up!/Word Wise and Word Work, the phonemic awareness/spelling and phonics stations, practice the same set of skills each week, so the stations can be adapted in similar ways. Encourage children to decode the words aloud with a partner. Use the following suggestions to adapt the phonemic awareness and phonics stations for English language learners.

- Be sure that children understand the meanings of all of the words before they use the stations.

- When possible, introduce any cognates or language transfer skills that will help children better understand the words practiced.

- Review the words or patterns using the Sound-Spelling Charts.

- Use one of the Picture Cards to model decoding the word.

- Write the word and point to the spellings of the word as you say each sound. Model blending each word.

- Have groups of mixed abilities use letter tiles to spell out the spelling words. Children should read the words they made to the other groups of children. Offer guidance as necessary.

Words to Know

English language learners can benefit in Words to Know, the vocabulary station, by using visuals and real objects to scaffold meaning. Children should be encouraged to use their home languages to transfer any vocabulary knowledge or strategies to what they are practicing. The following suggestions can be used to adapt the vocabulary station.

- Introduce any cognates or language transfer skills that will help children better understand the lesson vocabulary.

- Use visuals and gestures to review the meaning of high-frequency words.

- Revisit the high-frequency words with children daily. Help children say each word aloud and encourage oral production at other times during the school day.

- Have groups of mixed abilities work together using Letter Tiles to make their lesson vocabulary words. Have more advanced children model and define the words. Offer guidance as necessary.

Let's Write!

Children at all proficiency levels should be given a variety of materials they need to be able to write successfully. Some children may benefit from brainstorming and using graphic organizers while some may benefit by working independently with a writing prompt. The adaptations below may help your English language learners succeed in Let's Write!

- Provide sentence frames, writing prompts, or writing models to assist children's writing.

- For beginning and intermediate children, write out sentences they dictate. Allow them to copy the sentences and then read them aloud to you. Children can also draw a picture and label the different parts.

- More advanced children can write sentences and share with a partner.

Read for Meaning

Have a variety of Decodable, Leveled, ELL, and ELD Readers available at the comprehension station. Children may benefit from reviewing the comprehension skill with the Envision It! pictures in the Student Edition or the Picture It! blackline masters found in the *English Language Learner's Handbook*. The comprehension station may be adapted using the following suggestions.

- Use picture cues to review the comprehension skill.

- Choose a passage or selection that is appropriate to children's reading level. Read aloud the selection or passage with children.

- During reading, ask questions or fill out a graphic organizer with children to monitor their comprehension.

- Allow beginning and intermediate children to orally explain the relationships between the comprehension skill and the passage read. More advanced children can complete this activity by writing sentences.

Get Fluent

Guide children to determine the best fluency routine for them to use at this station. Be sure all children are practicing the different fluency traits with text at their levels and that they understand what they are reading. Adapt the fluency station for English language learners using the following suggestions.

- Have pairs of mixed-ability children reread the ELL or ELD Reader to each other or together.

- Circulate and evaluate intermediate to advanced children for word recognition, accuracy, and prosody.

- Work individually with beginning and intermediate children, focusing on decoding for meaning. Provide support as needed.

The Practice Stations provide valuable opportunities for children to gain knowledge and increase their confidence, thereby making their social and academic classroom experiences more meaningful. In addition, children's involvement in the stations will strengthen their performance in all areas of instruction, and their work in the stations will positively affect their ability to function as active and independent learners.

Assessing Station Activities

Using Assessment to Guide Instruction Informal, ongoing assessments are important means of guiding classroom instruction, and station activities provide excellent opportunities for ongoing assessments.

Station time is an extension of your lesson. It provides an opportunity for you to work with small groups, but it is not "busy time" for the other children. Station time provides a wonderful opportunity for you to assess how well children can apply what you have taught. The work they do during station time is an important piece of your assessment of the whole child!

There are many formal and informal ways to assess children and their work. Many of these assessments include children assessing their own work. Use the activities throughout the school year to measure children's growth and development.

The following assessment tools may be helpful as you informally assess children's station work.

Rubrics

- Create simple pictorial rubrics to guide children in assessing their own work.

- Use a rubric to guide your assessment of children's creativity and motivation.

Portfolios

- Save work children complete during station time. Use portfolio contents to measure children's progress and growth over time.

Informal Observations

- You may want to use a notebook or the Observation Record on page 17 to record your observations of children.

- Divide the class into small groups. Focus on observing a small group of children during station time each day instead of trying to observe all children's behaviors.

- Determine ahead of time what you will observe each week. Perhaps it is social interactions or emotional development. Some weeks you may wish to focus on academic development. Determining your expectations will help narrow your assessment.

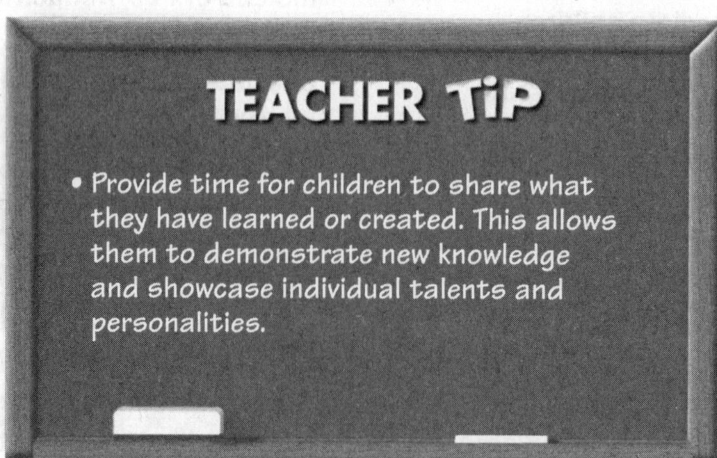

Observation Record

Date........................ Child..

Date........................ Child..

Date........................ Child..

Date........................ Child..

Date........................ Child..

Date........................ Child..

Student Work Plans

What Are Student Work Plans?

Pages 19–48 contain lesson-specific reproducible work plans for children to use during their independent activity time. Each work plan lists the tasks that children will complete, in stations or independently, while you meet with small groups. The work plans help children remember their assignments, plan their time, and keep track of what they've done. Work plans allow children to take responsibility and will aid them in becoming successful independent learners.

How Do I Use the Student Work Plans?

Begin by explaining the activities in the Practice Stations to children. Then distribute copies of *My Work Plan* and review the tasks. Be sure children understand that they will check the box next to each task as they complete it. Remind children that if they finish an activity before time is up, they should answer the Wrap Up Your Week questions or read silently. At the end of the week, you can collect children's work plans, or you can send them home.

If you prefer, you can customize a work plan for one or more children or for use during a particular lesson. For this purpose, a generic work plan can be found on p. 49.

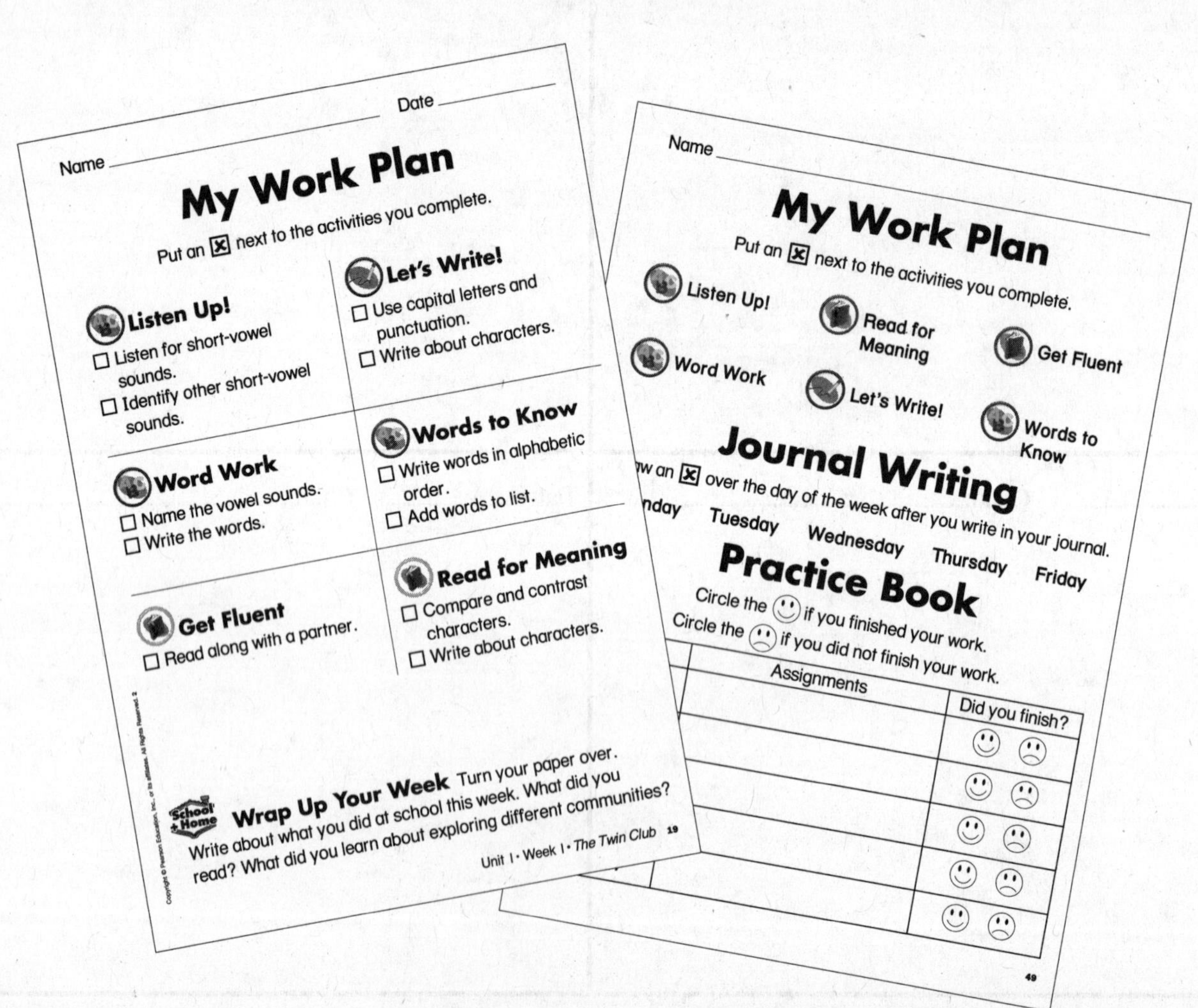

My Work Plan

Put an ☒ next to the activities you complete.

 ## Listen Up!

- ☐ Listen for short-vowel sounds.
- ☐ Identify other short-vowel sounds.

 ## Let's Write!

- ☐ Use capital letters and punctuation.
- ☐ Write about characters.

 ## Word Work

- ☐ Name the vowel sounds.
- ☐ Write the words.

 ## Words to Know

- ☐ Write words in alphabetic order.
- ☐ Add words to list.

 ## Get Fluent

- ☐ Read along with a partner.

 ## Read for Meaning

- ☐ Compare and contrast characters.
- ☐ Write about characters.

 **Wrap Up Your Week** Turn your paper over. Write about what you did at school this week. What did you read? What did you learn about exploring different communities?

My Work Plan

Put an ☒ next to the activities you complete.

 **Listen Up!**

☐ Identify words with constant and short vowel sounds.

 **Let's Write!**

☐ Use capital letters and punctuation.
☐ Write a personal narrative.

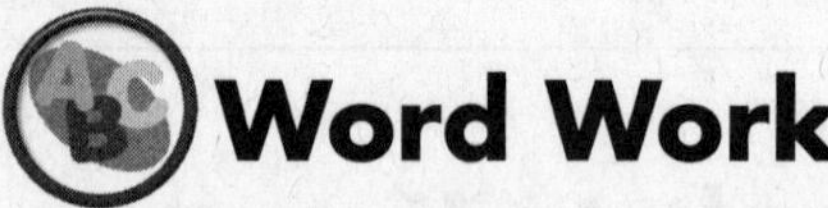 **Word Work**

☐ Sort words by sounds.

Words to Know

☐ Write words in alphabetic order.
☐ Add words to the list.

 **Get Fluent**

☐ Read along with a partner.

 **Read for Meaning**

☐ Identify setting.
☐ Compare and contrast different settings.

Wrap Up Your Week Turn your paper over. Write about what you did at school this week. What did you read? What did you learn about exploring space?

My Work Plan

Put an ☒ next to the activities you complete.

 ## Listen Up!

☐ Identify words with long-vowel sounds.

 ## Let's Write!

☐ Write expository nonfiction.
☐ Use variety of sentences.
☐ Include facts and details.

Word Work

☐ Build words.
☐ Write words.

Words to Know

☐ Draw a picture.
☐ Write sentences using position words.

 ## Get Fluent

☐ Read aloud with a partner.

 ## Read for Meaning

☐ Identify main idea and details.

Wrap Up Your Week Turn your paper over. Write about what you did at school this week. What did you read? What did you learn about exploring nature?

My Work Plan

Put an ☒ next to the activities you complete.

Listen Up!

- ☐ Say and blend sounds.
- ☐ Write words.

Let's Write!

- ☐ Write realistic fiction.
- ☐ Use transition words.

Word Work

- ☐ Sort words.

Words to Know

- ☐ Identify synonyms.

Get Fluent

- ☐ Read aloud with a partner.

Read for Meaning

- ☐ Identify the setting and character.
- ☐ Describe character.

School + Home

Wrap Up Your Week Turn your paper over. Write about what you did at school this week. What did you read? What did you learn about exploring the desert?

My Work Plan

Put an ☒ next to the activities you complete.

🅰🅱 Listen Up!

- ☐ Say and blend sounds.
- ☐ Write words.

✏ Let's Write!

- ☐ Write a brief report.
- ☐ Use describing words.

🅰🅱 Word Work

- ☐ Add endings to verbs.
- ☐ Use verbs in sentences.

🅰🅱 Words to Know

- ☐ Arrange words in alphabetic order.

📖 Get Fluent

- ☐ Read aloud with a partner.

📖 Read for Meaning

- ☐ Identify the main idea and details.

School + Home

Wrap Up Your Week Turn your paper over. Write about what you did at school this week. What did you read? What did you learn about searching for answers?

My Work Plan

Put an ☒ next to the activities you complete.

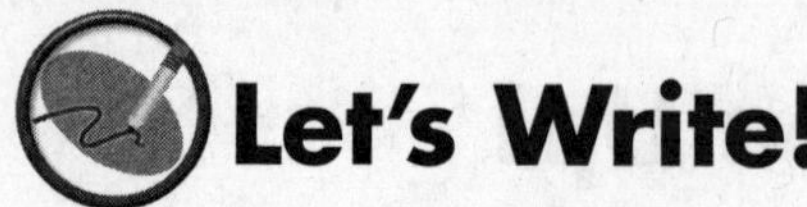 Listen Up!

- ☐ Say and blend sounds.
- ☐ Tell a story, a poem, or a riddle.

Let's Write!

- ☐ Write a scene for a play.
- ☐ Use the format of a play.

Word Work

- ☐ Say words.
- ☐ Make new word cards.

Words to Know

- ☐ Replace words with synonyms.

 Get Fluent

- ☐ Read aloud with a partner.

 Read for Meaning

- ☐ Identify facts.
- ☐ Identify details.

School + Home

Wrap Up Your Week Turn your paper over. Write about what you did at school this week. What did you read? What did you learn about helping others in danger?

My Work Plan

Put an ☒ next to the activities you complete.

 Listen Up!

- ☐ Substitute sounds to make new words.
- ☐ Use words in a story, poem, or a riddle.

 Let's Write!

- ☐ Write a narrative nonfiction story.
- ☐ Include your feelings.

 Word Work

- ☐ Write words.
- ☐ Circle the vowel-*r* sound.

 Words to Know

- ☐ Use context clues.
- ☐ Draw a picture.

 Get Fluent

- ☐ Read aloud with a partner.

 Read for Meaning

- ☐ Identify causes and effects.
- ☐ Use a graphic organizer.

School + Home

Wrap Up Your Week

Turn your paper over. Write about what you did at school this week. What did you read? What did you learn about working together to change history?

My Work Plan

Put an ☒ next to the activities you complete.

 **Listen Up!**

- ☐ Count the number of sounds.
- ☐ Match words with same number of sounds.

 **Let's Write!**

- ☐ Write a biography.
- ☐ Include key events and qualities about the person.

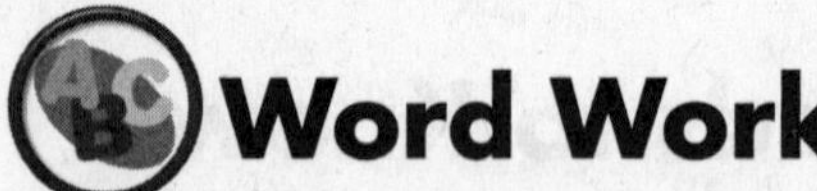 **Word Work**

- ☐ Spell contractions.
- ☐ Write words that make up contractions.

Words to Know

- ☐ Write guide words.
- ☐ Make a glossary.

 **Get Fluent**

- ☐ Read aloud with a partner.

Read for Meaning

- ☐ Write the author's purpose.
- ☐ Write supporting details.

Wrap Up Your Week Turn your paper over. Write about what you did at school this week. What did you read? What did you learn about working together?

My Work Plan

Put an ☒ next to the activities you complete.

Listen Up!

☐ Make new words.
☐ Say words.

Let's Write!

☐ Write a nonfiction story.

Word Work

☐ Spell words.
☐ Write words.

Words to Know

☐ Identify sequence.
☐ Use time-order transition words.

Get Fluent

☐ Read aloud with a partner.

Read for Meaning

☐ Write facts.
☐ Write details.

School + Home

Wrap Up Your Week Turn your paper over. Write about what you did at school this week. What did you read? What did you learn about working together and working alone?

My Work Plan

Put an ☒ next to the activities you complete.

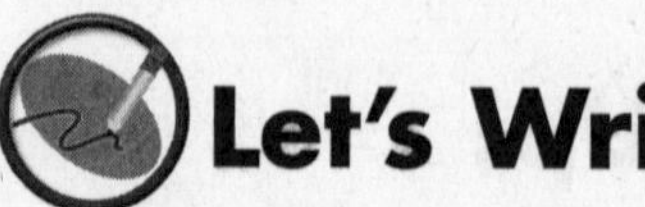

Listen Up!

☐ Make new words.

Let's Write!

☐ Write a fairy tale.
☐ Write a beginning, a middle, and an end.

Word Work

☐ Identify plural endings.
☐ Write plurals.

Words to Know

☐ Write using homophones.

Get Fluent

☐ Read aloud with a partner.

Read for Meaning

☐ Identify causes and effects.
☐ Fill in the graphic organizer.

Wrap Up Your Week Turn your paper over. Write about what you did at school this week. What did you read? What did you learn about how we can contribute to a celebration?

My Work Plan

Put an ☒ next to the activities you complete.

 **Listen Up!**

☐ Make new words.
☐ Change final sounds.

 **Let's Write!**

☐ Vary sentence beginnings.
☐ Write a folk tale.

 **Word Work**

☐ Make new word cards.

 **Words to Know**

☐ Use context clues.
☐ Write a synonym.

Get Fluent

☐ Read aloud with a partner.

 **Read for Meaning**

☐ Use a graphic organizer.
☐ Compare and contrast characters or things.

Wrap Up Your Week Turn your paper over. Write about what you did at school this week. What did you read? What did you learn about inventors and their inventions?

My Work Plan

Put an ☒ next to the activities you complete.

 ## Listen Up!

☐ Change final sound of words to make new words.

 ## Let's Write!

☐ Write an animal fantasy.
☐ Vary characters' personalities.

Word Work

☐ Make word cards for new words.
☐ Use words in a poem.

Words to Know

☐ Identify antonyms.
☐ Use antonyms in a sentence.

 ## Get Fluent

☐ Read aloud with a partner.

 ## Read for Meaning

☐ Write the author's purpose.
☐ Write supporting details.

Wrap Up Your Week Turn your paper over. Write about what you did at school this week. What did you read? What did you learn about ways we communicate?

My Work Plan

Put an ☒ next to the activities you complete.

 **Listen Up!**

☐ Change the middle sound of words.

 **Let's Write!**

☐ Write a friendly letter.
☐ Stick to the main topic.

 **Word Work**

☐ Make new word cards for words.
☐ Use words in a poem.

Words to Know

☐ Add prefixes to words.

 **Get Fluent**

☐ Read aloud with a partner.

Read for Meaning

☐ Write a conclusion.
☐ Write details and facts that support your conclusion.

Wrap Up Your Week Turn your paper over. Write about what you did at school this week. What did you read? What did you learn about good and bad creative ideas?

My Work Plan

Put an ☒ next to the activities you complete.

Listen Up!

☐ Identify words with three, four, and five sounds.

Let's Write!

☐ Write a narrative poem.
☐ Use capital letters.
☐ Use verbs correctly.

Word Work

☐ Make new compound words.

Words to Know

☐ Identify antonyms.
☐ Draw a sentence.

Get Fluent

☐ Read aloud with a partner.

Read for Meaning

☐ Compare and contrast characters.

Wrap Up Your Week Turn your paper over. Write about what you did at school this week. What did you read? What did you learn about creative ways to solve problems?

Name _______________________________   Date ___________

My Work Plan

Put an ☒ next to the activities you complete.

Listen Up!

- ☐ Change final sounds to make new words.
- ☐ Draw a picture.

Let's Write!

- ☐ Write a realistic fiction story.
- ☐ Use details.
- ☐ Write a beginning, middle, and end.

Word Work

- ☐ Make word cards for new words.
- ☐ Use words in a story.

Words to Know

- ☐ Identify words from other languages.
- ☐ Draw and label a picture.
- ☐ Write sentences.

Get Fluent

- ☐ Read aloud with a partner.

Read for Meaning

- ☐ Write the sequence of events.

Wrap Up Your Week Turn your paper over. Write about what you did at school this week. What did you read? What did you learn about from where creative ideas come?

My Work Plan

Put an ⊠ next to the activities you complete.

 **Word Wise**

- ☐ Spell words with endings.

 **Let's Write!**

- ☐ Write a review.
- ☐ Include a main idea and details.

 **Word Work**

- ☐ Add endings to words.
- ☐ Write sentences.

 **Words to Know**

- ☐ Identify synonyms.
- ☐ Write sentences or a paragraph using synonyms.

 **Get Fluent**

- ☐ Read aloud with a partner.

 **Read for Meaning**

- ☐ Fill out a graphic organizer.
- ☐ Identify facts and opinions.

Wrap Up Your Week Turn your paper over. Write about what you did at school this week. What did you read? What did you learn about how familiar things can help us with change?

My Work Plan

Put an ☒ next to the activities you complete.

 ## Word Wise

- ☐ Write sentences.
- ☐ Underline *-le* words.
- ☐ Make picture cards.

 ## Let's Write!

- ☐ Write a letter.
- ☐ Include reasons and persuasive details.

 ## Word Work

- ☐ Make new word cards.
- ☐ Underline the *-le* words.
- ☐ Write a poem.

 ## Words to Know

- ☐ Write definitions of words.
- ☐ Check meanings.
- ☐ Use words in sentences.

 ## Get Fluent

- ☐ Read aloud with a partner.

 ## Read for Meaning

- ☐ Write a conclusion.
- ☐ Write supporting details and facts.

Wrap Up Your Week Turn your paper over. Write about what you did at school this week. What did you read? What did you learn about how seeds grow?

My Work Plan

Put an **☒** next to the activities you complete.

 ## Word Wise

- ☐ Match cards and sounds.
- ☐ Sort words into a chart.
- ☐ Write a story.

 ## Let's Write!

- ☐ Write a nonfiction story.
- ☐ Use vivid or descriptive words.

 ## Word Work

- ☐ Match sounds and cards.
- ☐ Say words.
- ☐ Write words.

 ## Words to Know

- ☐ Identify antonyms.
- ☐ Write a sentence.
- ☐ Fill out a chart.

Get Fluent

- ☐ Read aloud with a partner.

 ## Read for Meaning

- ☐ Identify sequence of events.

Wrap Up Your Week Turn your paper over. Write about what you did at school this week. What did you read? What did you learn about changes that occur underground?

My Work Plan

Put an ☒ next to the activities you complete.

Word Wise

☐ Spell words.
☐ Sort words in a chart.

Let's Write!

☐ Write a report about soil.
☐ Combine sentences.

Word Work

☐ Match cards and sounds.
☐ Write new words.

Words to Know

☐ Define words with suffixes.
☐ Write words.
☐ Make new words.

Get Fluent

☐ Read aloud with a partner.

Read for Meaning

☐ Write opinions.
☐ Write supporting facts.

Wrap Up Your Week Turn your paper over. Write about what you did at school this week. What did you read? What did you learn about difficult changes?

My Work Plan

Put an **☒** next to the activities you complete.

 ## Word Wise

- ☐ Spell words.
- ☐ Write sentences.
- ☐ Sort words by vowel sounds.

 ## Let's Write!

- ☐ Write a poem about changes.
- ☐ Use sensory details.

 ## Word Work

- ☐ Circle vowel teams.
- ☐ Write new words.

 ## Words to Know

- ☐ Write definitions.
- ☐ Write sentences.

 ## Get Fluent

- ☐ Read aloud with a partner.

 ## Read for Meaning

- ☐ Write the plot.
- ☐ Write the theme.

Wrap Up Your Week Turn your paper over. Write about what you did at school this week. What did you read? What did you learn about how weather changes affect us?

My Work Plan

Put an ☒ next to the activities you complete.

 Word Wise

- ☐ Sort words into columns.
- ☐ Circle the diagraphs.
- ☐ Write new words.

Let's Write!

- ☐ Write a thank-you note.

 Word Work

- ☐ Draw and write.
- ☐ Sort words in columns.

 Words to Know

- ☐ Add prefixes to words.
- ☐ Write sentences.

 Get Fluent

- ☐ Read aloud with a partner.

 Read for Meaning

- ☐ Write the plot and theme.

Wrap Up Your Week Turn your paper over. Write about what you did at school this week. What did you read? What did you learn about why it is important to do a good job?

My Work Plan

Put an ☒ next to the activities you complete.

Word Wise

- ☐ Spell words with suffixes.
- ☐ Sort words into columns.

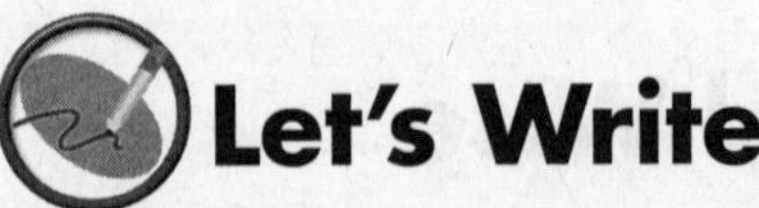
Let's Write!

- ☐ Write story about a job.
- ☐ Use details and vivid words.

Word Work

- ☐ Write words with suffixes.

Words to Know

- ☐ Add suffixes to words.
- ☐ Write sentences.

Get Fluent

- ☐ Read aloud with a partner.

Read for Meaning

- ☐ Write an opinion.
- ☐ Write supporting facts.

School + Home **Wrap Up Your Week** Turn your paper over. Write about what you did at school this week. What did you read? What did you learn about being a responsible community member?

My Work Plan

Put an ☒ next to the activities you complete.

 ## Word Wise

☐ Spell words with prefixes.
☐ Write sentences.

 ## Let's Write!

☐ Write a story about a hero.
☐ Write events in sequence.

 ## Word Work

☐ Add prefixes to words.

Words to Know

☐ Look up words in a dictionary.
☐ Write sentences.

 ## Get Fluent

☐ Read aloud with a partner.

 ## Read for Meaning

☐ Use graphic organizer to list causes and effects.
☐ Write a paragraph.

Wrap Up Your Week Turn your paper over. Write about what you did at school this week. What did you read? What did you learn about being a responsible family member?

My Work Plan

Put an ⊠ next to the activities you complete.

Word Wise

- ☐ Spell words with silent letters.
- ☐ Sort words into columns.

Let's Write!

- ☐ Write a journal entry.
- ☐ Use details and vivid words.

Word Work

- ☐ Write words with silent letters.
- ☐ Write sentences.

Words to Know

- ☐ Sort words into categories.
- ☐ Check a dictionary.

Get Fluent

- ☐ Read aloud with a partner.

Read for Meaning

- ☐ Write a review.
- ☐ Summarize the plot.
- ☐ Write the theme.

Wrap Up Your Week Turn your paper over. Write about what you did at school this week. What did you read? What did you learn about responsibility to friends and neighbors?

My Work Plan

Put an ☒ next to the activities you complete.

 ## Word Wise

☐ Spell words.
☐ Write words in a chart.

 ## Let's Write!

☐ Write a fantasy about animals.
☐ Use pronouns and quotation marks.

 ## Word Work

☐ Draw and label picture.
☐ Sort and write words.

 ## Words to Know

☐ Identify the smaller words in a compound word.
☐ Write sentences.

 ## Get Fluent

☐ Read aloud with a partner.

 ## Read for Meaning

☐ Write about the setting.
☐ Write about the main characters.

Wrap Up Your Week Turn your paper over. Write about what you did at school this week. What did you read? What did you learn about what happens when we do the wrong thing?

My Work Plan

Put an ☒ next to the activities you complete.

 Word Wise

☐ Spell words.
☐ Sort words in a chart.

 Let's Write!

☐ Write a funny story.
☐ Vary sentences.

 Word Work

☐ Say words.
☐ Draw and write words.

 Words to Know

☐ Define words with suffixes.
☐ Write sentences.

Get Fluent

☐ Read aloud with a partner.

Read for Meaning

☐ Write a paragraph.
☐ Tell the main idea.

School + Home **Wrap Up Your Week** Turn your paper over. Write about what you did at school this week. What did you read? What did you learn about the importance of sports in our country?

My Work Plan

Put an ☒ next to the activities you complete.

 ## Word Wise

☐ Spell words with endings.
☐ Circle the endings.
☐ Write sentences.

 ## Let's Write!

☐ Write a story.
☐ Include a beginning, a middle, and an end.

 ## Word Work

☐ Write words with endings.

Words to Know

☐ Use homophones in sentences.
☐ Make a poster.
☐ Write a story or scene.

 ## Get Fluent

☐ Read aloud with a partner.

 ## Read for Meaning

☐ Compare and contrast characters.

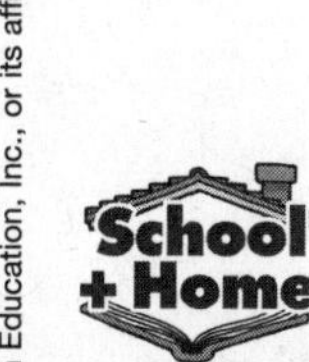

Wrap Up Your Week
Turn your paper over. Write about what you did at school this week. What did you read? What did you learn about what our flag means?

My Work Plan

Put an ☒ next to the activities you complete.

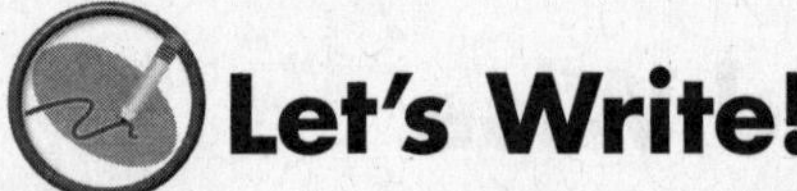 Word Wise

- ☐ Write abbreviations.
- ☐ Write sentences.

Let's Write!

- ☐ Write a song or poem about traditions.

 Word Work

- ☐ Match abbreviations and words.
- ☐ Write sentences.

 Words to Know

- ☐ Use context clues.
- ☐ Write sentences.

Get Fluent

- ☐ Read aloud with a partner.

Read for Meaning

- ☐ Write the author's purpose.
- ☐ Use supporting details.

School + Home

Wrap Up Your Week Turn your paper over. Write about what you did at school this week. What did you read? What did you learn about what makes family celebrations special?

My Work Plan

Put an ☒ next to the activities you complete.

 ## Word Wise

- ☐ Draw and write sentences.
- ☐ Write new words.

 ## Let's Write!

- ☐ Write an invitation.
- ☐ Illustrate the invitation.

 ## Word Work

- ☐ Make picture cards.
- ☐ Write sentences.

 ## Words to Know

- ☐ Draw and label a picture.
- ☐ Write sentences.

 ## Get Fluent

- ☐ Read aloud with a partner.

Read for Meaning

- ☐ Draw a conclusion.
- ☐ Use supporting details.

School + Home **Wrap Up Your Week** Turn your paper over. Write about what you did at school this week. What did you read? What did you learn about cowboys?

My Work Plan

Put an ☒ next to the activities you complete.

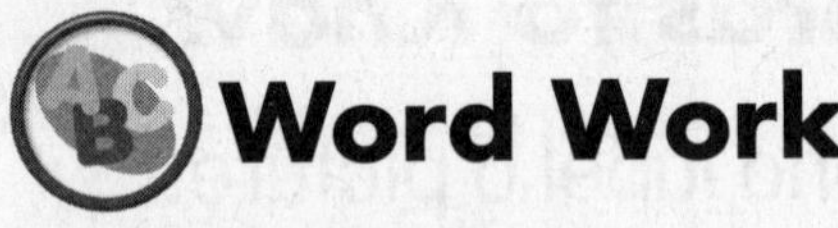 Word Wise

☐ Spell words with suffixes.
☐ Write sentences.

 Let's Write!

☐ Write about chores.
☐ Compare and contrast the chores.

 Word Work

☐ Fill out chart.

Words to Know

☐ Use context clues.
☐ Write a paragraph.

 Get Fluent

☐ Read aloud with a partner.

 Read for Meaning

☐ Draw and label the sentence.
☐ Make a time line.

Wrap Up Your Week Turn your paper over. Write about what you did at school this week. What did you read? What did you learn about the many ways people can celebrate?

My Work Plan

Put an ☒ next to the activities you complete.

 **Listen Up!**

 **Read for Meaning**

 **Get Fluent**

 **Word Work**

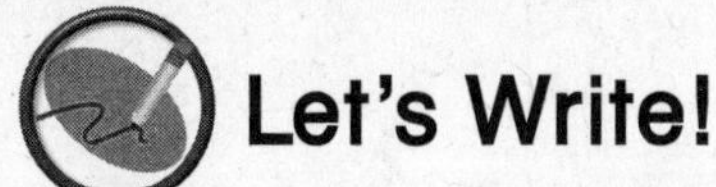 **Let's Write!**

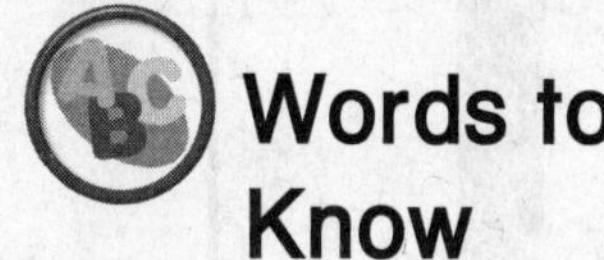 **Words to Know**

Journal Writing

Draw an ☒ over the day of the week after you write in your journal.

Monday   Tuesday   Wednesday   Thursday   Friday

Practice Book

Circle the ☺ if you finished your work.

Circle the ☹ if you did not finish your work.

	Assignments	Did you finish?
Monday		☺ ☹
Tuesday		☺ ☹
Wednesday		☺ ☹
Thursday		☺ ☹
Friday		☺ ☹

What Can I Do?

1

2

3

4